ANIMAL BATTLES

HUMMINGBIRD VS. MOTH

BY NATHAN SOMMER

TORQUE™

TORQUE, AN IMPRINT OF BELLWETHER MEDIA BY FLUTTERBEE

Torque brims with excitement perfect for thrill-seekers of all kinds. Discover daring survival skills, explore uncharted worlds, and marvel at mighty engines and extreme sports. In *Torque* books, anything can happen. Are you ready?

This edition first published in 2027 by Bellwether Media, Inc.

For information regarding permission, write to Bellwether Media, Inc., Attention: Permissions Department, 3500 American Blvd W, Suite 150, Bloomington, MN 55431.

Library of Congress Cataloging-in-Publication Data is available at www.loc.gov or upon request from the publisher.

ISBN: 9798898801137 (hardcover)
ISBN: 9798898802721 (paperback)
ISBN: 9798898802370 (ebook)

Editor: Suzane Nyguen Designer: Josh Brink

Printed in the United States of America, North Mankato, MN.

TABLE OF CONTENTS

THE COMPETITORS

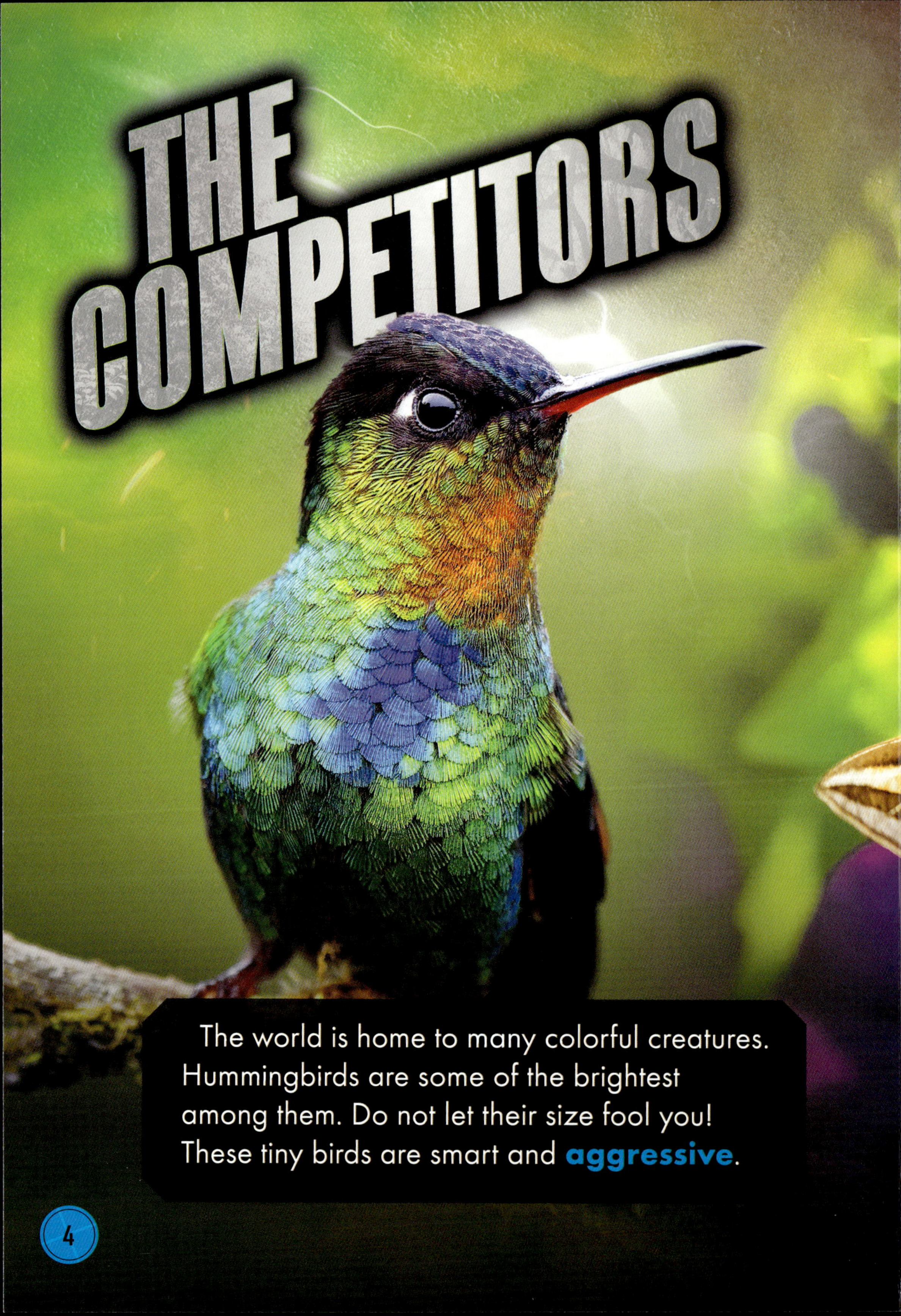

The world is home to many colorful creatures. Hummingbirds are some of the brightest among them. Do not let their size fool you! These tiny birds are smart and **aggressive**.

Hummingbirds compete for nectar with moths. These **insects** have many interesting **adaptations** to avoid or scare off enemies. Which winged competitor will win?

Hummingbirds are named after the humming sound their flight creates. They have colorful bodies with bladelike wings and long, skinny bills. Females are often larger with duller colors than males.

Hummingbirds live across North and South America. Most prefer deserts, gardens, and woodlands. They build nests from plants and twigs woven with spider silk.

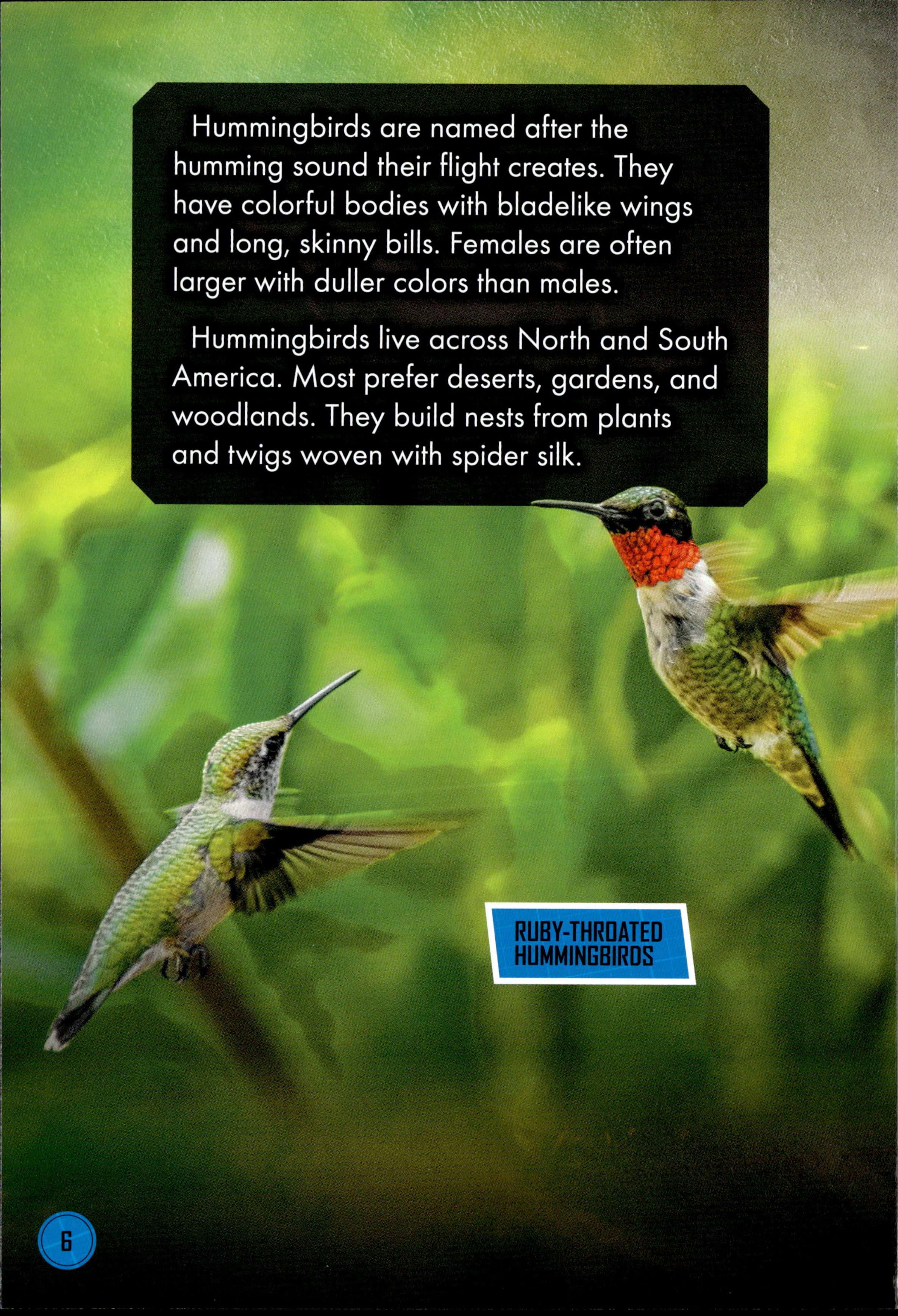

RUBY-THROATED HUMMINGBIRDS

RUBY-THROATED HUMMINGBIRD PROFILE

WINGSPAN

UP TO 4.7 INCHES
(12 CENTIMETERS)

LENGTH

UP TO 3.75 INCHES
(9.5 CENTIMETERS)

HABITATS

FORESTS

GARDENS

RUBY-THROATED HUMMINGBIRD RANGE

WHITE-LINED SPHINX MOTH PROFILE

WINGSPAN

UP TO 3.5 INCHES
(8.9 CENTIMETERS)

LENGTH

2 INCHES
(5 CENTIMETERS)

HABITATS

WOODLANDS

GARDENS

WHITE-LINED SPHINX MOTH RANGE

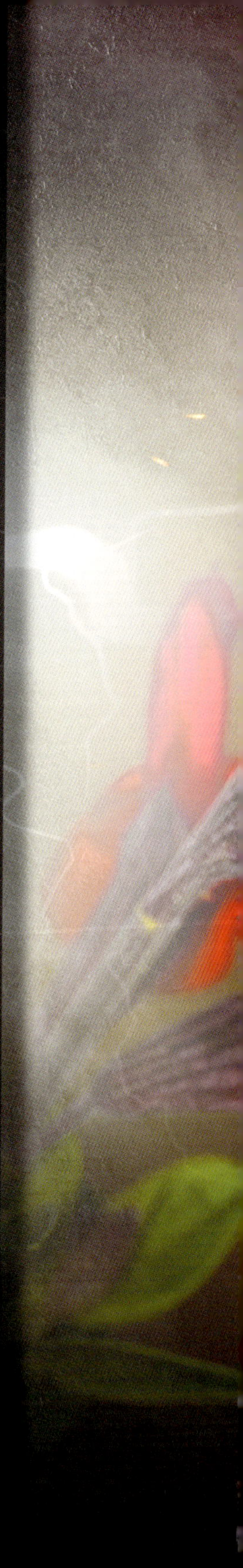

Moths are insects closely related to butterflies. Most have thick, fuzzy bodies and feather-like **antennae**. They have two sets of scale-covered wings. The wings often have bright colors and patterns.

There are around 160,000 moth **species**. The largest have 14-inch (36-centimeter) wingspans. These insects can survive in most **habitats**. They are found everywhere except Antarctica.

STAGES OF LIFE

Moths hatch from eggs as caterpillars. Most enter silk cocoons to grow into adults.

SECRET WEAPONS

THE SMALLEST BIRD

Bee hummingbirds are the world's smallest bird. They are around 2 inches (5 centimeters) long.

Flexible joints make hummingbirds excellent flyers. They can fly straight up and down and sideways. They can also fly backwards. These birds can easily catch insects mid-flight!

Moths use **camouflage**. Many use patterned wings to blend in with leaves and twigs. Some moth wings have **eyespot** markings that look like large animal eyes. Some moths can make themselves look like spiders, snakes, or wasps. This scares enemies away.

Large hearts give hummingbirds a lot of energy. They can beat their wings up to 80 times per second! Some fly more than 30 miles (48 kilometers) per hour. Some can travel for 20 hours without stopping.

TOP SPEED

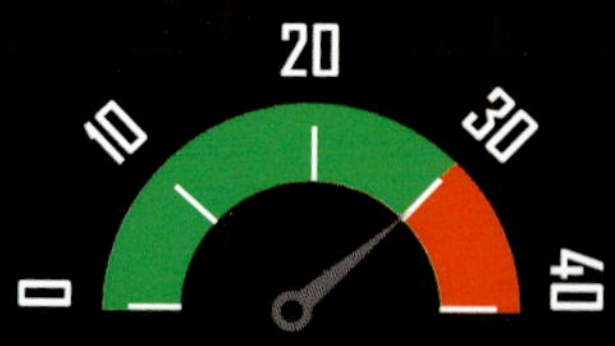

HUMMINGBIRD SPEED
30 MILES
(48 KILOMETERS) PER HOUR

FASTEST HUMAN
28 MILES
(45 KILOMETERS) PER HOUR

Moth wings have overlapping scales. These help them absorb sound waves. They block the **echolocation** bats use to hunt them. This makes moths almost invisible to bats.

SECRET WEAPONS

HUMMINGBIRD

FLEXIBLE JOINTS

HIGH ENERGY

SHARP BILL

SWORD-BILLED HUMMINGBIRD BILL

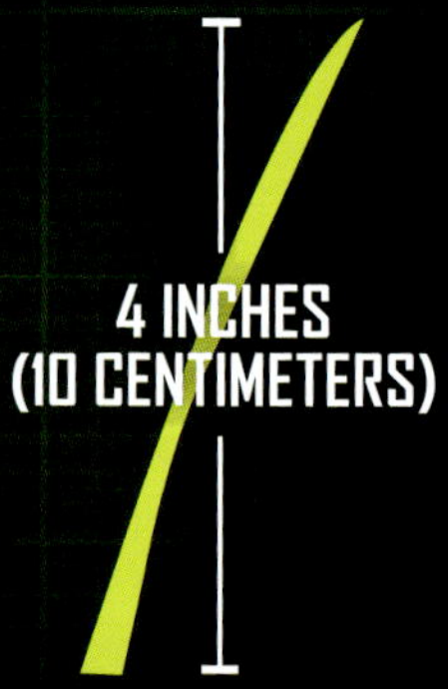

Hummingbird bills are long and sharp. The birds use these as weapons and to easily reach into flowers. Their bills have forked tongues inside. They flick these many times to lap up nectar quickly.

SECRET WEAPONS

MOTH

CAMOUFLAGE

SOUND-BLOCKING SCALES

TOXIC CHEMICALS

Many moths are **toxic**. They produce **chemicals** that make them smell and taste bad. This causes **predators** to avoid eating the insects.

ATTACK MOVES

Hummingbirds mostly eat nectar. They also catch insects by surprise. Many fly through groups to capture insects in their mouths. Others pluck insects from leaves and branches.

Most adult moths have a liquid diet. They eat nectar from flowers and juices from fruits. They use straw-like feeding tubes in their mouths to eat.

CATERPILLAR DIET

Most moth caterpillars eat plants. Some hunt insects and even other caterpillars!

FREQUENT FEEDERS

Hummingbirds eat about every 15 minutes. They can eat half their body weight in one day.

Hummingbirds are aggressive fighters. They often dive-bomb enemies headfirst. Then they stab them with their bills. Some rip the feathers off other birds!

Many moths use **scare tactics** against enemies. They flash their wings to show their bright colors and large eyespots. They quickly zigzag in different directions to escape startled predators.

READY, FIGHT!

A hummingbird spots a moth drinking nectar. It dive-bombs the moth. But the moth flashes its eyespots! This does not scare the bird.

The moth tries to blend in on a leaf. The bird spots the moth. The hummingbird stabs at the moth with its bill. The hurt moth flies away in a zigzag. The hummingbird has won today!

GLOSSARY

adaptations—changes in animals over time that make them better able to hunt and survive

aggressive—ready to fight

antennae—long, thin body parts on the heads of insects used to smell and feel

camouflage—colors and patterns used to help an animal hide in its surroundings

chemicals—materials that can cause a change in other materials

echolocation—a way of locating objects using reflected sound waves

eyespot—a spot of color on the wings of moths that look like eyes

flexible—able to bend easily

habitats—the homes or areas where animals prefer to live

insects—small animals with six legs and hard outer bodies; an insect's body is divided into three parts.

predators—animals that hunt other animals for food

scare tactics—fighting strategies in which animals try to make themselves appear as large or scary as possible in hopes of scaring other animals off

species—kinds of animals

toxic—unpleasant or harmful to one's health

TO LEARN MORE

AT THE LIBRARY

Dell, Pamela. *Hummingbird*. Mankato, Minn.: Creative Education, 2026.

Emminizer, Theresa. *Insect Life Cycles*. Buffalo, N.Y.: Enslow Publishing, 2025.

Langdo, Bryan. *Butterflies and Moths: Friends of Flowers*. Minneapolis, Minn.: Bearport Publishing Company, 2026.

ON THE WEB

FACTSURFER

Factsurfer.com gives you a safe, fun way to find more information.

1. Go to www.factsurfer.com.
2. Enter "hummingbird vs. moth" into the search box and click .
3. Select your book cover to see a list of related content.

INDEX

The images in this book are reproduced through the courtesy of: Melody Mellinger, front cover (hummingbird); Cathy Keifer, front cover (moth); emer1940, pp. 2 (flowers), 3 (flowers), 20 (flowers), 21 (flowers), 22 (flowers), 23 (flowers), 24 (flowers); Isolde, pp. 2 (moth), 3 (moth), 20 (moth), 21 (moth), 22 (moth), 23 (moth), 24 (moth); ND STOCK, pp. 2 (hummingbird), 3 (hummingbird), 20 (hummingbird), 21 (hummingbird), 22 (hummingbird), 23 (hummingbird), 24 (hummingbird); phototrip.cz, pp. 4, 14 (hummingbird); Susan Hodgson, p. 5; Fiona M. Donnelly, pp. 6-7, 16; Jim, pp. 8-9; mlharing, p. 10; alessandrozocc, p. 11; Barbora Polivkova, p. 12; Dominyk Lever, p. 13; petrsalinger, p. 14 (flexible joints); Stewart, p. 14 (high energy); Luc Pouliot, p. 14 (sharp bills); Eric Dale Creative, p. 15 (camouflage); Bernard, p. 15 (sound-blocking scales); ViniSouza128, p. 15 (toxic chemicals); Ira Mark Rappaport, p. 15 (moth); Nigel Harris, p. 17; ZacksPhoto, p. 18; ArmadilloGrafix, p. 19.